ENGINEERING IN ACTION

ELECTRICAL ENGINEERING

AND THE Science of Circuits

Crabtree Publishing Company

www.crabtreebooks.com

James Bow

Crabtree Publishing Company

www.crabtreebooks.com

Author: James Bow
Publishing plan research and development:
  Sean Charlebois, Reagan Miller
  Crabtree Publishing Company
Photo research: James Nixon
Editors: Paul Humphrey, Adrianna Morganelli,
  James Nixon
Proofreader: Kathy Middleton
Layout design: sprout.uk.com
Cover design and logo: Margaret Amy Salter
Production coordinator and prepress
  technician: Margaret Amy Salter
Print coordinator: Katherine Berti

Produced for Crabtree Publishing Company
by Discovery Books

Photographs:
Alamy: pp. 5 (H. Mark Weidman Photography), 13 top
  (Everett Collection Historical), 14 (Pictorial Press Ltd),
  17 bottom-right (Stephen Morrison/EPA), 20 (Blend
  Images), 24 (Peter Bowater), 25 (Photo-Stock Israel).
Bobby Humphrey: p. 26.
Brookhaven National Laboratory: p. 17 left.
Corbis: p. 12 (Schenectady Museum; Hall of Electrical
  History Foundation).
Shutterstock: cover (bottom left), pp. 4 left (BMJ), 4
  bottom-right (Carlos E. Santa Maria), 6 top (Yevgeniy
  Steshkin), 6 bottom (Lonely), 7 (oksana 2010), 8
  (MilanB), 15 bottom (Art Studio), 16 top (Senkaya), 16
  bottom (Nomad Soul), 28 (Dotshock).
Thinkstock: cover (all except bottom left)
Wikimedia: pp. 9 right (Chris Darling), 9 bottom-left
  (Walter Larden), 10 (Philadelphia Museum of Arts), 11
  top (Harriet Moore), 11 bottom (Universal Studios/Dr.
  Macro), 13 bottom, 15 top (Michael Holley), 18
  (Ontario Power Generation), 19, 21 right (Napoleon
  Sarony), 21 left (Dickenson V. Alley), 22, 23 top, 23
  middle (Ensign John Gay, U.S. Navy), 23 bottom
  (Courtesy of the Naval Surface Warfare Center/U.S.
  Naval Historical Center), 27 (Tucker M. Yates), 29
  (NASA).

Library and Archives Canada Cataloguing in Publication

Bow, James, 1972-
    Electrical engineering and the science of circuits / James Bow.

(Engineering in action)
Includes index.
Issued also in electronic formats.
ISBN 978-0-7787-7497-6 (bound).--ISBN 978-0-7787-7502-7 (pbk.)

    1. Electrical engineering--Juvenile literature. 2. Electric
circuits--Juvenile literature. I. Title. II. Series: Engineering in
action (St. Catharines, Ont.)

TK148.B69 2012   j621.3   C2012-906845-4

Library of Congress Cataloging-in-Publication Data

CIP available at Library of Congress

Crabtree Publishing Company

www.crabtreebooks.com   1-800-387-7650

Printed in the U.S.A./092014/CJ20140801

Published in Canada
Crabtree Publishing
616 Welland Ave.
St. Catharines, ON
L2M 5V6

Published in the United States
Crabtree Publishing
PMB 59051
350 Fifth Avenue, 59th Floor
New York, New York 10118

Published in the United Kingdom
Crabtree Publishing
Maritime House
Basin Road North, Hove
BN41 1WR

Published in Australia
Crabtree Publishing
3 Charles Street
Coburg North
VIC, 3058

CONTENTS

AN ELECTRIFYING SUBJECT

If you are reading this, chances are electricity is an important part of your life. You may be using a light bulb to read this book by. Your home has a furnace to keep you warm and a refrigerator to keep your food cold. You have a telephone to talk to friends. You have a radio or a television or a computer to bring you news. If you go out, streetlights light your way and traffic lights keep vehicles moving safely. Without electricity, none of these things would be possible.

What is electrical engineering?: Electrical engineers are involved with all aspects of electricity. They know how to make electricity, how to bring it to where it's needed, how to store it, and how to make it work for us. They help build power stations and design transmission lines that carry electrical power from place to place, and signals that make our phones and Internet work. They work with some of the biggest machines, such as airplanes, and the smallest, such as the circuit boards in computers.

Transmission lines take electricity from where it's made to where it's used.

Electrical engineers help make the instrument panels that tell these pilots how the plane is flying.

Science and engineering: Scientists understand why electricity exists. Electrical engineers are the mechanics who design the machines that use electricity. Engineers understand the complex processes that take place in some of the smallest things in the universe, and they are always exploring further, looking for ways to make a difference in the world. Electrical engineers follow an eight-step process to design, build, and test new machines:

1. Start with a problem or task that has to be done

↓

2. Work out the requirements of the task

↓

3. Brainstorm ways of tackling the problem or task

↓

4. Choose the best possible method

↓

5. Make a model of the new item

6. Test the model to see how well it works

7. Improve the design if testing shows any problems

↓

8. Get people working on the new design

Electrical engineers design the circuit boards that make computers work.

EARLY SHOCK THERAPY

Some of the earliest electrical engineers were doctors from ancient Greece. Noticing that electric shocks numbed the body, they suggested patients suffering from headaches should touch electric fish to their heads to numb their pain.

ELECTRICITY— NATURE'S POWER

Lightning is electricity. A bolt of lightning can heat the air hotter than the sun. A strike lasts for less than a second but contains enough electricity to power a light bulb for months. Imagine—something so powerful comes from some of the smallest bits of matter in the universe.

All charged up!

Electricity comes from **electrons**. Electrons are part of **atoms**, the tiny particles of matter that help make up everything around us. Electrons orbit, or circle, an atom's nucleus, or middle, in rings called shells. Electrons naturally have a charge, or an energy that attracts them like magnets to an opposite charge at the nucleus of the atom.

Some atoms, especially in metals, gain or lose electrons easily. These changes in the number of electrons make the atom's charge unbalanced. The atom becomes attracted to other atoms or electrons that have the opposite charge. When the charged particles (atoms, electrons) move from one place to another, this makes a flow called an **electric current**.

Lightning strikes Earth over eight million times a day.

Electrons move around the nucleus of the atom.

6

Charged particles move better through some things, such as wire, than others, such as air. When the difference in an unbalanced charge builds up enough, electrons find a way of reaching an opposite charge, resulting in a blast of power. Lightning is the result of electrons in storm clouds jumping to the opposite-charged ground. It can also strike within or between clouds.

Electricity flows into the copper wires of a motor, making them magnetic. This pushes against magnets surrounding the motor, making the motor turn.

Electricity and magnetism:

If the way opposite charges attract reminds you of how magnets work, you're not alone. In the 19th century, British scientist Michael Faraday saw that electricity and magnetism are connected. Electricity can move magnets, and magnets can be moved over wires to make electricity. This is how **generators** (machines that make electricity) work: just as motors use magnets to turn electricity into movement, generators use magnets to turn movement into electricity.

MAKING IT WORK

Not only can electricity move magnets to turn motors, it can be used to send signals quickly to places far away. The challenge for electrical engineers is understanding how to control electricity. How do we make it? And how do we make it work for us?

YOUR OWN LIGHTNING

Electricity even moves inside your body. Ions (charged atoms)—including sodium, potassium, and chlorine—create the current that makes your nerves spark and your muscles move.

CONNECTING ELECTRICITY AND MAGNETISM

Let's show how electricity and magnetism are linked.

Like charges repel: Take two lengths of tape about four inches (10 cm) long. Stick them on a smooth plastic surface and then pull them off quickly. Now try to touch their non-sticky sides together. You will notice that the two strips seem to want to get away from each other (repulsion).

Static electricity is an electric charge trapped on the surface of an object. When tape is peeled off a smooth surface, it gathers electrons (static electricity), which give it a negative charge. The two pieces of tape with negative charges are attracted only to positive charges, not each other. They push each other apart, just like magnets do. Magnets are materials that produce a magnetic field around them, which can attract or repel other magnets.

The two ends of a magnet are called poles. Earth itself is a magnet, with a North Pole and a South Pole.

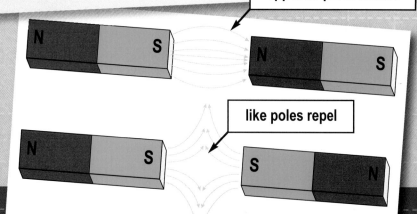

opposite poles attract

like poles repel

Opposites attract: This time, place the sticky part of one piece of tape onto the non-sticky part of the other. Blow on them along their length. This **neutralizes** the charge. Then, pull them apart quickly. Bring the two non-sticky sides close together without having them touch. You will find that the two pieces of tape now want to touch (attraction).

When you pull two pieces of tape apart, the electrons don't come away equally. One piece of tape becomes more positive and the other more negative. Because opposite charges attract, the pieces pull together, like magnets.

Note: The tape experiments work best on cold, dry days because differences in charge go away more slowly. Humid air is a better conductor than dry air, meaning charges move through moist air more easily and balance themselves more quickly. For the same reason, you are more likely to get a shock from rubbing your socks on the carpet in winter than in summer.

The plastic of a playground slide gives up electrons easily. They go into your hair as static electricity.

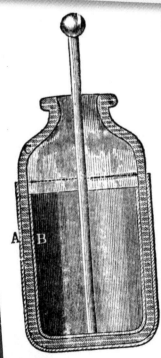

THE LEYDEN JAR

Although Ewald Georg von Kleist made the discovery first in 1745, it was Pieter van Musschenbroek who is given credit for creating the world's first **capacitor**—a device for building up and storing an electrical charge. Van Musschenbroek lined the inside and outside of a glass jar with foil, then added water and a metal rod sticking down from the top. This would become known as a Leyden jar. The jar was much simpler and easier to use than the large electrostatic generators scientists had been using before to study electricity.

HOW THE SPARK WAS FOUND

For as long as people have been on Earth, we've known about lightning and been in awe of its power. We also knew that electricity existed elsewhere, too. The ancient Egyptians discovered an electric eel and named it "Thunderer of the Nile." Around 600 BCE, the Greek philosopher Thales of Miletos observed sparks made from rubbing amber rods against cats' fur and realized electricity was something we could make happen. He also saw that the rubbed rods could attract light objects, like feathers.

From curiosity to something useful
In the late 1500s, Dr. William Gilbert, a physician for England's Queen Elizabeth I, repeated Thales' experiments with amber and found other things that could spark when rubbed. He created the first device that could detect these sparks—a spinning needle. He named the force "electricity." Other scientists learned ways to make electricity on demand. Otto von Guericke built the first electrostatic generator in 1660.

Benjamin Franklin's kite: Franklin's famous kite, flown during a thunderstorm in 1752, was not actually struck by lightning—that would have killed him. Simply flying a kite through enough layers of air will naturally generate an electrical charge on its own. Franklin's dangerous experiment did, however, prove the connection between lightning and electricity.

It wasn't until the 19th century that scientists began to understand what they were working on. George Ohm began measuring electric current in 1827, and the unit of electric **resistance** now bears his name. Six years earlier Michael Faraday made a wire dipped in mercury spin around a magnet using an electric charge. This experiment and others helped Faraday and his partner James Clark Maxwell connect electricity to magnetism. This moved electricity from being a curiosity to something that could make things move, and more scientists joined the field to explore what was possible. By the 1880s, the first university programs in electrical engineering began.

Michael Faraday works in his laboratory. His experiments changed the way we thought about electricity, magnetism, and light.

BAGHDAD BATTERY

One of the earliest electrical devices may have come from ancient Iraq. The Baghdad battery, as it was called, was a clay pot dating from 250 BCE, believed to have held crushed grapes, an iron bar, and a copper wire.

Scientists found that the pot would have generated a small electric charge—hardly enough to feel, but enough, perhaps, to put a thin film of copper or gold on a cheap statue made of tin—a process called electroplating.

IT'S ALIVE!

Around 1810, Mary Shelley watched a sideshow performer shock a dead body with electricity, making it jump and jerk. The experience inspired her to write the novel Frankenstein, in which electricity is used to bring a human monster to life.

ELECTRICITY CHARGES THE WORLD

Electricity traveled very fast and could be used to send signals. Electric telegraphs were devices that sent electricity through wires to machines that could decode them into messages. In 1858, Britain's Queen Victoria and U.S. President Buchanan sent each other the first telegraph messages to cross the Atlantic Ocean. By that time, a telegraph network had been established across the United States.

Scientists also made electricity move things. Working from Faraday's experiment making an electrified wire move around a magnet, British scientist William Sturgeon invented, in 1832, the first electric motor able to power tools. By the 1880s, these motors were moving the first electric trains.

An electric locomotive in 1895 draws power from the wires and sends it to a motor which turns the wheels.

Electrical terms:

Ampere (amp): a measure of how much electrical charge passes through a circuit in a certain time

Volt: a measure of the charge available

Watt: a measure of how much work an electric charge can do. We figure this by the amount of charge available (volt) and how much charge can pass through a circuit in time (ampere).

The great inventor

One person who improved the technology was Thomas Edison. In 1876, he used his fortune to build a **research laboratory** in Menlo Park, New Jersey, to study how electricity could be used. His work helped to launch or improve inventions such as the telephone, the phonograph (record player), the electric motor, and the light bulb. He built the world's first electrical network, providing 110 volts of current to customers in lower Manhattan, New York, powering other inventions of his that people were now buying.

The 1893 Columbian Exposition in Chicago showed off electric lights at night.

THOMAS EDISON (1847-1931)

Thomas Edison's first job was selling newspapers to train passengers in Michigan, but he spent his spare time experimenting with chemicals and electricity. He received his first patent—for an electric voice recorder—in 1869. By 1931, he had 1,093 patents, for inventions such as the record player, the movie camera and projector, and devices that helped the telephone to work. His work on telegraphs and electric transmission changed our cities through the early part of the 20th century.

Contrary to popular belief, Edison did not invent the light bulb. That happened 50 years earlier. However, he did improve it so it worked well enough and was cheap enough to be put in people's homes.

SMALLER, FASTER, CHEAPER, BETTER

By the 1890s, electric light let people work after dark more easily, electric railroads moved people farther, and telegraphs sent messages faster. The quality of life in North America and Europe improved. But inventive electrical engineers didn't stop there.

The Colossus *computing machine helped Britain break Nazi codes in World War II.*

In 1895, Italian Guglielmo Marconi invented the radio, which could send and receive electric signals without wires. Inventors also added electricity to mechanical calculators, making the first electronic computing machines and, in the 1940s, the first mainframe computers.

Electricity goes to war: The military helped develop electronic technologies. RADAR bounced radio signals off enemy aircraft to show where they were flying, helping Britain defend itself against Nazi air attack during World War II. Colossus, an electronic computing device, translated complex German codes, allowing the British military to figure out where the enemy was before they attacked.

These inventions needed electricity to be carefully controlled. In the early part of the 20th century, the only device that could do this was a vacuum tube, which looked like a light bulb. Electrical devices needed lots of vacuum tubes. This made them large and heavy.

Smaller is better

In 1947, American **physicists** William Shockley, John Bardeen, and Walter Brattain invented the transistor—a device that worked like a vacuum tube did, but in a size smaller than a fingertip. Electrical devices could now be made smaller. The first **microprocessor** in 1968 packed thousands of transistors into a 12-inch (30-cm) by two-inch (five-cm) space. As transistors got even tinier, computers became many times smaller and more powerful.

This was the size of an electric calculator in 1972. Today's machines can do the same work but are a fraction of the size.

An electrical engineer works on a circuit board, making electrical connections between the tiny parts by melting soft metal. The transistors on the board turn the electricity into useful signals.

MOORE'S LAW

In 1965, Gordon Moore observed that the number of transistors in electronic devices doubled every two years. Through the 1990s and 2000s, many devices followed Moore's law, doubling speed and space for data storage. We are reaching the limits of how small or powerful we can make electronic devices, however, as transistors approach the size of atoms. A future challenge for electrical engineers will be getting around this limit, making machines as small as atoms, or computers smart enough to think for themselves.

ELECTRICAL ENGINEERS AT WORK

Today, over 300,000 people work as electrical engineers in the United States. There are 37,000 electrical engineers in Canada. Their skills are required in many industries, and they use a wide set of skills on the job.

An electrical engineer fixes a generator

Below left: An electrical engineer adds a heat sink to a computer processor. This device absorbs unwanted heat that could damage the computer's circuits.

Useful to so many people: You will find electrical engineers working for computer hardware companies designing circuit boards. You will find them at power stations helping to build and maintain the generators there. Telephone companies and radio stations need electrical engineers to help build their towers or transmission lines. Electrical engineers work on the engine and the dashboard displays of cars. Nothing that uses a circuit board, from the computers in your home to the air traffic-control systems at airports, will work without electricity.

Electrical engineers need to know the chemical and physical reactions that make electricity. They need good math skills to understand how electricity moves and what things move electricity best. They need to know how to use computers, since computers are becoming even more important in designing electrical devices today.

WOMEN IN ELECTRICAL ENGINEERING

It may seem from the history section of this book that all electrical engieers were men. However, many women have also contributed to the advances of electrical engineering:

Edith Clarke (1883-1959): first female electrical engineer in the U.S. Worked at General Electric and taught at the Electrical Engineering Department at the University of Texas.

Caroline Haslett (1895-1957): learned electrical engineering while working for the Cochran Boiler Company in the U.K. In the early 1920s, worked toward increasing the use of electric lights and heating in U.K. homes. Co-founded the Electrical Association of Women.

Elsie MacGill (1905-1980): first Canadian woman to have a degree in electrical engineering. During World War II, managed a staff of 4,500 workers, building over 2,000 fighter aircraft.

Dr. Veena Rawat: became first female doctor in electrical engineering in Canada in 1973. Worked in the field of **radio communications**. Chaired organizations regulating the industry and championed the increase of women in science and technology.

Claire Gmachl: graduated from the University of Innsbruck, Austria, in 1991. Designs some of the most powerful and complex lasers in the world.

Claire Tomlin: graduated from the University of Waterloo, Canada, in 1992. Currently the director of the Hybrid Systems Laboratory at the University of California, Berkeley. Designs unmanned aerial vehicles and air traffic-control systems.

Without electrical engineers, air traffic controllers wouldn't have complex displays to help them keep track of planes and prevent them from crashing into each other.

Claire Gmachl prepares one of her lasers.

ELECTRICAL ENGINEERS SOLVE PROBLEMS

Like other engineers, electrical engineers are problem solvers. The first step in solving a problem is identifying exactly what the problem is in the first place.

What is the problem?

If something is broken—like a downed transmission wire causing a blackout or a bad connection causing a machine to catch fire—that's a problem. But some problems are harder to spot than that.

In the early part of the 20th century, **visionaries** like Sir Adam Beck saw that the electrical network was limited to cities. People in the countryside didn't have electricity. It wasn't because something was broken, but Beck saw that it was a problem. He and people like him saw electricity as a basic service that every person should have.

The Sir Adam Beck Generating Complex at Niagara Falls uses water pressure to make enough electricity to power a million homes each year.

Identify criteria and constraints:

Once you identify the problem, you must find out what is needed to solve the problem. The criteria are the requirements your project must meet. The constraints are the things that limit what you can engineer, and you need to understand these, too.

For Sir Adam Beck, the problem would be solved once electricity came to farms. The limits he faced were the costs of generating the power and the difficulty of getting an electrical wire out to each and every farm. It was also important to know the dangers of something going wrong, like construction accidents or downed wires.

Electrical engineers must solve a problem in a way that's easy, inexpensive, and safe.

SIR ADAM BECK

Sir Adam Beck was a Canadian politician who took up the cause of making cheap electricity available to as many people as possible. To solve this problem, he founded the Hydro-Electric Power Commission of Ontario, which began work building a power station that used the rushing water of Niagara Falls to turn turbines and create a lot of electricity. He convinced politicians to pay for transmission lines to send this electricity far and wide, to cities and farms alike.

The power stations at Niagara Falls are named Sir Adam Beck 1 and 2 in his honor. In Canada people still call their home electricity "hydro." The work of visionaries like Beck made electricity a part of everybody's lives throughout North America.

BRAINSTORMING AND EXPLORING

Once electrical engineers know what the problem is, they must gather ideas on how to solve it. One way to do this is by brainstorming. Here, engineers get together and write down ideas on how to solve a problem. They look at what worked before and think of things they haven't tried. At this point, no idea is too unusual. The more ideas people come up with, the more likely they will find one that leads to the solution.

Once all the ideas have been gathered, it's time to explore the possibilities of those ideas. Will they work? Can they be done with the tools at hand?

*Two electrical engineers brainstorm on a project about **wind turbines**. Working as a team generates more ideas than working alone.*

No idea too unusual: Thomas Edison's groundbreaking electrical network set up in 1882, provided 110 volts of direct current (DC) to his customers. DC worked well with light bulbs, but it didn't travel well. Customers far from generators lost power. After some brainstorming, Edison tried to solve this by building smaller power plants closer to customers. This proved expensive.

Then, in 1887, Edison had a challenger. Nikola Tesla gained a patent for a different method of delivering electricity named alternating current (AC). To Edison, this idea was madness.

AC versus DC: Direct current travels one way through a wire, whereas alternating current switches direction rapidly. Tesla knew AC was easier to generate, and it could be safely sent down wires at higher voltages to customers farther from the generator. The voltage (number of volts) is a measurement of the amount of work that has to be done to move an electric charge between two points.

Edison fought to keep DC as the standard, even advertising fatal accidents that occurred with AC, but Tesla's ideas won out. Today, almost all power systems use AC.

NIKOLA TESLA (1856-1943)

Nikola Tesla was a Serbian-American physicist whose ideas helped in the invention of radio and electrical transmission. He liked working with powerful currents and explored moving electricity without wires.

Like Edison, he was always brainstorming new ideas, sometimes before he identified problems to solve. Later in life, he claimed to have built a "death ray," which used a blast of powerful electricity to bring down planes, but never showed it to the public. This gave him a reputation as a "mad scientist."

Nikola Tesla invented the Tesla coil, seen here at his Colorado Springs laboratory in 1899. It makes artificial lightning.

FROM DRAWING BOARD TO PROTOTYPE

After selecting an approach from the brainstormed ideas, electrical engineers don't just apply it to the problem and expect it to work. Ideas that are good in theory may not work well in practice, and it is better to discover this using a **prototype**, or a model, rather than on a full-sized machine.

A "breadboard" lets electrical engineers test different circuit patterns in the real world.

Test runs: In the early part of the 20th century, electrical engineers made circuit-board prototypes from "breadboard"– a block of plastic full of holes, with metal clips inside each hole. Electrical engineers could fit wires into these holes without **solder,** making it easy to test circuit designs and fix bugs before they become problems.

Sometimes, bigger prototypes are needed. Engineers at car companies often build full-sized prototype vehicles–right down to the wiring–to test and re-test before they are happy with the design. Any problems are looked at by the design engineers, then corrections are made, and the prototype is rebuilt to be tested again. Most industries, including the aviation industry, test full-scale prototypes of new designs, especially when flaws in the design could have deadly consequences.

Computer-aided design:

Today, computer-aided design allows engineers to draw designs without pencil and paper, and 3-D printers allow them to produce plastic models of their designs that can be tested. Computers can **simulate** how a device will work without building it in the real world. If something doesn't work, they can change the design in the computer and try again.

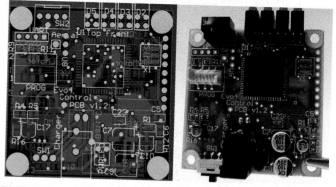

A computer-aided design (on the left) allows electrical engineers to plan and test a circuit design before the real one (on the right) is built.

New plane designs have to be taken on test runs by pilots with nerves of steel. There can be risks in building and testing prototypes.

SHOCK THERAPY

Sometimes ideas are rushed into use without proper testing. Shock therapy was developed in the 1940s, to treat mental illness by applying electric shocks to the brain. Doctors using this technique didn't really know what they were doing. Today shock therapy is known as ECT (electroconvulsive therapy). Using smaller charges placed more carefully in the brain, it now helps to treat many forms of mental illness.

THE FIRST BUG

In the 1940s, computer pioneer Grace Hopper was tracing an error inside a computing machine and found a moth had been caught in one of the switches, causing the problem. She taped the moth to the official report on the error, and this led to all other computer errors being called "bugs."

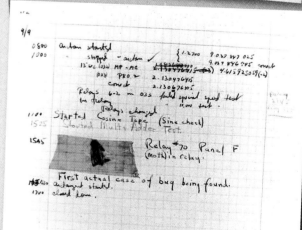

MAKING IT WORK

Once the prototype has been tested, it's time for electrical engineers to share their results. The company that owns the design produces it and sends the product to stores where people buy it. Sometimes the design is communicated to the general public. Simple designs for generating power may mean that people in poor areas far from electrical lines can light their homes without spending a lot of money, so sometimes solutions are made available for free, for the good of all.

If the process has been followed carefully, the machines built from the design will work, and the problem will be solved.

BLACKOUT!

Electricity always wants to find its way to the ground. It doesn't sit still in wires, and it can only be safely stored in **batteries**. Most power is used within a second of it being generated. Power supply must match demand, or the system can shut down. On July 30, 2012, large parts of India lost power when an overused power station shut down. The disruption spread throughout the national network leaving 670 million people without power!

Power stations are being built in developing countries such as India to meet a growing demand for electricity.

Back to the drawing board: When the final design is built the process doesn't end there. Mistakes can happen, even after careful testing. A badly wired circuit board can overheat and catch fire. A faulty instrument panel can send the wrong information to a pilot and cause a plane to crash. A computer error can shut a power station down, causing a blackout.

Nobody likes mistakes, but when they happen, engineers can learn from them. Engineers look at what went wrong and improve the design.

Also, technology is improving all the time, which means better ways of doing things become available that weren't available before. When this happens, these improvements can be added to the design, making the solution cheaper and better for the people who use it.

SHORT CIRCUIT MEANS FIRE

In 2007, 250,000 Maytag brand washing machines had to be recalled in North America. because of a potential fire hazard. The company eventually had to pay the families whose homes had been put at risk. The mistake cost the company millions.

DESIGN CHALLENGE: MAKE A TELEGRAPH

You want to send messages to your friends, but your computer and telephone are being used by someone else in your family. You do have buzzers, batteries, wire, and tape, as well as blocks of wood, screws, and paper clips. Can you build your own telegraph network? Approach this like an electrical engineer.

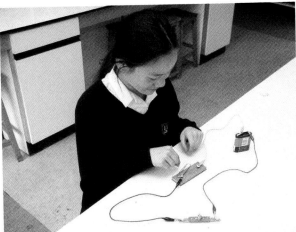

1: Identify the need or problem: You want to send messages to your friends by other means than your phone or computer.

2: Identify requirements and constraints: Figure out what it means to solve the problem. You want your friends to receive signals from you. The message has to be clear and understood. You are constrained by the materials at hand.

3: Brainstorm!: You have a battery and a buzzer. How does the buzzer help? Remember that electric currents travel down wires very fast. Write down your ideas.

4: Choose a solution: Look at your ideas and see what works with what you have at hand.

5: Construct a prototype: Try connecting the battery to the buzzer using two lengths of wire. To create a circuit, one wire should go from one end of the battery to one contact of the buzzer, and the other wire should go from the other contact of the buzzer to the other end of the battery.

MORSE CODE

In 1836, before sound could be sent over wires, American Samuel Morse designed a code of long and short electric charges, known as dashes and dots, to send signals through wires that others could translate into letters.

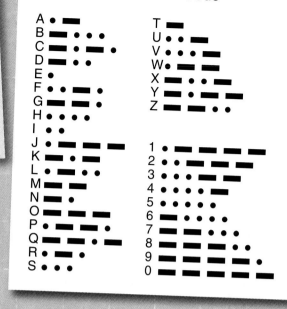

International Morse Code

A	• ▬		T	▬
B	▬ • • •		U	• • ▬
C	▬ • ▬ •		V	• • • ▬
D	▬ • •		W	• ▬ ▬
E	•		X	▬ • • ▬
F	• • ▬ •		Y	▬ • ▬ ▬
G	▬ ▬ •		Z	▬ ▬ • •
H	• • • •			
I	• •		1	• ▬ ▬ ▬ ▬
J	• ▬ ▬ ▬		2	• • ▬ ▬ ▬
K	▬ • ▬		3	• • • ▬ ▬
L	• ▬ • •		4	• • • • ▬
M	▬ ▬		5	• • • • •
N	▬ •		6	▬ • • • •
O	▬ ▬ ▬		7	▬ ▬ • • •
P	• ▬ ▬ •		8	▬ ▬ ▬ • •
Q	▬ ▬ • ▬		9	▬ ▬ ▬ ▬ •
R	• ▬ •		0	▬ ▬ ▬ ▬ ▬
S	• • •			

7: Improve the design: Does the signal have to be a buzzer? Can you use a light bulb instead? And does the signal have to be off and on? Could you add more wires and more lights, and switches to move electricity from one wire to another?

6: Test your prototype: Ouch! The buzzer is now buzzing loudly and not stopping. Can you make the electricity turn off and on when you need it to? What does turning the buzzer off and on mean? Can you and your friends make up a code?

8: Communicate the design: Tell your friends. Write up your project. Use diagrams to show others how they can make what you've made. Ask them if they can improve on the design.

DANGER: SHORT CIRCUIT

DO NOT run a wire directly from a positive contact to a negative one on a battery. That causes a **short circuit**, which can overheat the battery and cause it to explode.

FUTURE CHALLENGES

Thanks to electrical engineers we can talk to people on the other side of the world, work late into the night, and move faster than we ever have before. But challenges exist for the future.

Where will our electricity come from? Most of our electricity is made by burning coal and oil to heat water and using the steam to turn turbines inside generators. Coal and oil are **non-renewable** resources. As they run out, it will be harder to keep the lights on.

Collecting the sun's energy is a challenge for engineers. Thirty-four percent of the sun's energy that hits Earth just bounces back into space.

Also, our power stations aren't keeping up with our growing cities. In August 2003, heavy power use overloaded an Ohio power station. The disruption ripped through the system until 30 million people across the northeastern U.S. and parts of Canada were without power.

One solution may be to look for alternative energy sources. Some engineers are designing wind turbines, which use wind to turn generators. Others are developing solar cells, which change the sun's energy into electricity to power homes without the need of a big power grid. These are already in place in some homes and communities.

Doing more with less: If we are to power our homes from home, or just use less energy from the grid, then we need to make our household devices do more with less electricity. Efficient refrigerators and washing machines already save us money as well as reduce our need for power. After decades of using Edison's light bulb, electrical engineers designed light-emitting diodes (LEDs) that turn less electricity into more light.

Into space: As we send robots and satellites out to explore space, electrical engineers are challenged to make machines do more work with less power. In August 2012, NASA's robot named Curiosity landed on Mars and began exploring its surroundings and sending information back to Earth. This laboratory is powered by a **nuclear** battery that weighs less than 11 pounds (five kilograms).

Sometimes it seems like there are always new problems to be solved. For electrical engineers, however, these are just reasons to explore new ideas and come up with new solutions that will change the world.

The Curiosity rover uses a small nuclear battery as it moves around Mars, scoops up soil, performs experiments, and radios data back to Earth. The battery generates enough power to light a single 100-watt light bulb, and can last 15 years.

HARVESTING LIGHTNING

The power in lightning has led some to wonder if they could catch it. In 2007, a company tried using giant capacitors to absorb the electricity and release it to the power grid over time. However, the amount of power they were able to harvest was too small to make money. Even within thunderstorms, there's no guarantee where lightning will strike.

LEARNING MORE

BOOKS

Lynette, Rachel, *Electrical Experiments: Electricity and Circuits*, Heinemann Library, 2008

Oxlade, Chris, *Making a Circuit*, Raintree, 2012

Pegis, Jessica, *What are Insulators and Conductors?*, Crabtree, 2012

Sobey, Ed, *Electric Motor Experiments*, Enslow Publishers, 2012

Woodford, Chris, *Electricity: Investigating the Presence and Flow of Electric Charge*, Rosen Central, 2012

ONLINE

www.discoverengineering.org
Learn about engineering, take part in activities, play games, and do experiments.

http://users.stargate.net/~eit/kidspage.htm
Try simple experiments in electrical engineering at home.

www.opg.com/education/grades5-8/
Learn about electricity and how it is made.

http://electronics.howstuffworks.com/capacitor.htm
Find out how capacitors work.

http://pbskids.org/zoom/activities/sci/lemonbattery.html
Make your own battery at home.

http://pbskids.org/zoom/activities/sci/
Other fun experiments in engineering that you can do at home.

PLACES TO VISIT

Sir Adam Beck Generating Station, Niagara Falls, Ontario:
www.niagaraparks.com/attractions/sir-adam-beck.html

Thomas Edison Birthplace Museum, Milan, Ohio:
www.tomedison.org

Manitoba Electrical Museum & Education Centre, Winnipeg:
www.museevirtuelvirtualmuseum.ca/GetMuseumProfile.do?lang=en&chinCode=guabks

GLOSSARY

atom One of the smallest pieces of matter from which molecules, and all things, are made

battery A device that uses a chemical reaction between metals and acid to produce or store an electric charge

capacitor A device used to store an electric charge

electric current A flow of electrically charged particles, often carried in a wire

electrons A tiny particle that makes up part of an atom

generator A machine that turns movement into electricity. Coal or oil can be burned to boil water into steam and create the movement in a generator. Water in moving rivers can also do this.

microprocessor The part of the computer that does computing work, contained on a single chip

neutralize To make something neutral, canceling out differences

non-renewable Something that doesn't replace itself when it is used. Something that can be used up.

nuclear Having to do with the nucleus (core) of an atom

patent A legal document to show that an inventor owns an invention

physicist A scientist who studies physics—the study of nature, matter, and energy

prototype A model that is used to test a design before it is put into production

radio communications The study of sendingand receiving radio signals

research laboratory A place where scientists study and experiment, and look for new ways of doing things or understanding things

resistance When something blocks something else

short circuit When the positive and negative parts of a power source are connected by something with low resistance, like a wire, delivering a lot of energy in a short time. This can cause fire or explosions.

simulate To make something act as in the real world, but not actually for real

solder A metal that melts at low heat and can be used to join wires together

transmission Moving energy from place to place, such as power or signals

turbine The part of a generator that turns against magnets to generate electricity

visionary Somebody who sees something that does not yet exist and works hard to bring it about

wind turbine A tall structure with a spinning blade that converts the energy of the wind into electricity

INDEX